How to Draw the Life and Times of
Theodore Roosevelt

Frances E. Ruffin

The Rosen Publishing Group's
PowerKids Press™
New York

To my father, David C. Ruffin Jr.

Published in 2006 by The Rosen Publishing Group, Inc.
29 East 21st Street, New York, NY 10010

First Edition

Editor: Daryl Heller
Layout Design: Albert B. Hanner, Greg Tucker
Photo Researcher: Jeffrey Wendt

Illustrations: All illustrations by Albert Hanner.
Photo Credits: Cover, pp. 9, 12, 16, 22 Library of Congress Prints and Photograph Division; p. 4 © AP/Wide World Photos; pp. 7, 14 (bottom) © Getty Images; p. 8 Photograph courtesy of Eastern National, © 2005; pp. 10, 24 © Corbis; p. 14 (top) Theodore Roosevelt Collection, Harvard College Library; p. 18 From the original painting by Mort Künstler, The Rough Riders. ©1984 Mort Künstler, Inc. www.mkunstler.com; p. 20 © Bettmann/Corbis; p. 26 Sagamore Hill National Historic Site, National Park Service; p. 28 The White House Collection, courtesy the White House Historical Association.

Library of Congress Cataloging-in-Publication Data

Ruffin, Frances E.
  How to draw the life and times of Theodore Roosevelt / Frances E. Ruffin.— 1st ed.
    p. cm. — (A kid's guide to drawing the presidents of the United States of America)
  Includes index.
  ISBN 1-4042-3002-5 (library binding)
  1. Roosevelt, Theodore, 1858–1919—Juvenile literature. 2. Presidents—United States—Biography—Juvenile literature. 3. Drawing—Technique—Juvenile literature. I. Title. II. Series.

E757.R94 2006
973.91'1'092—dc22

                                    2005001552

Printed in China

Contents

Young Theodore

Theodore Roosevelt, America's twenty-sixth president, was shy as a child. As an adult he became a powerful force in U.S. politics. Theodore was the second of four children born to Theodore and Martha Bulloch Roosevelt in New York City, on October 27, 1858. The Roosevelt family arrived in America from Holland in the 1600s. By the mid-1900s, the Roosevelts were among the richest families in New York. Theodore's grandfather and father became millionaires in the real estate business and as merchants of plate glass, which was used for storefronts.

Theodore had a happy childhood, but he suffered from asthma, a lung condition that can make breathing hard. The asthma made him weak and sickly. Theodore's father told his son that he had a good mind, but he also needed to build a strong body. Theodore took boxing lessons, and his father built a gym in the family's New York City home where Theodore lifted weights and hit punching bags.

From early childhood Theodore loved and studied nature. He observed birds and other animals and kept a variety of creatures as pets, including snakes, turtles, and mice. Theodore kept notebooks about his pets. His nature studies became a lifelong hobby.

All the Roosevelt children were tutored, or taught by a private teacher, at home. When Theodore planned to go to Harvard University his parents hired a Harvard graduate to help Theodore prepare for the college's entrance tests. Theodore spent two years studying for six to eight hours a day. He passed the tests and was accepted into Harvard University.

You will need the following supplies to draw the life and times of Theodore Roosevelt:

✓ A sketch pad   ✓ An eraser   ✓ A pencil   ✓ A ruler

These are some of the shapes and drawing terms you need to know:

Horizontal Line	—		Squiggly Line	
Oval	⬭		Trapezoid	
Rectangle	▭		Triangle	△
Shading			Vertical Line	❘
Slanted Line	╱		Wavy Line	

The Twenty-sixth President

Before he became president, Theodore Roosevelt served in several public and political posts. In 1882, he became a New York state assemblyman. He later served as U.S. civil service commissioner, president of the board of the New York City Police Department, and assistant secretary of the navy. When William McKinley ran as the Republican candidate for president in 1900, Roosevelt was his vice-presidential running mate. They won. Ten months later Leon Czolgosz, an anarchist, assassinated McKinley in Buffalo, New York. Roosevelt was sworn in as U.S. president on September 14, 1901, at the age of 42.

As president, Roosevelt fought for laws to control how large corporations did business. He protected the environment by setting aside land for the creation of national forests, parks, and game preserves. Roosevelt also oversaw the construction of the Panama Canal, a waterway in Central America that would help the United States' trade and military interests. In 1904, Roosevelt was elected as president.

President Theodore Roosevelt was photographed around 1902 speaking before a crowd in Evanston, Illinois. Roosevelt was the youngest person ever to become a U.S. president.

Theodore Roosevelt's New York

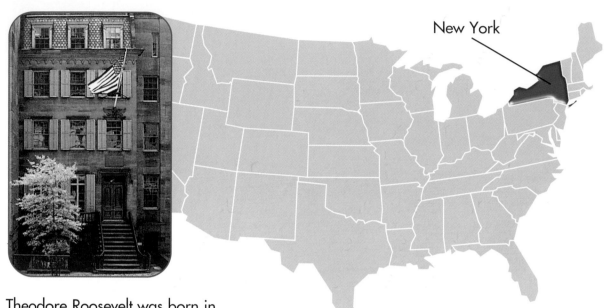

Theodore Roosevelt was born in this New York City brownstone.

Map of the United States of America

New York

Theodore Roosevelt was born at 28 East Twentieth Street in New York City, New York. His home was a five-story brownstone. A brownstone gets its name from the brown stones used to build it. Theodore's family lived there until he was 14 years old. Today visitors to Roosevelt's birthplace can see the family's furniture and paintings. The entrance floor contains photographs, medals, and papers that record Roosevelt's life.

In 1873, Theodore's father rented a summer home at Oyster Bay, on New York's Long Island. In 1880,

Roosevelt and his first wife, Alice, bought land near his parents' home. Roosevelt began building a summer vacation home on the property in 1884. Roosevelt called the house Leeholm after his first wife's maiden name, Lee. He later changed the name to Sagamore Hill when the 22-room house was completed in 1887. The new name came from a Native American chief whose nation had once lived on the land. Today people can see rooms that house the more than 6,000 books the Roosevelts collected. Both Sagamore Hill and Theodore Roosevelt's birthplace in New York City are managed by the National Park Service.

This is the Trophy Room at Sagamore Hill, which is the Roosevelts' estate on Oyster Bay, Long Island. The Trophy Room has mounted animal heads and animal skins that Roosevelt collected while hunting. This was the Roosevelts' favorite room.

A Harvard Man

Theodore Roosevelt entered Harvard University in the fall of 1876. He lived at 16 Winthrop Street, near the Cambridge, Massachusetts, campus. Roosevelt chose Harvard because he thought that he wanted a career in science. Harvard had a strong program in the natural sciences, as well as many science teachers who were well known in the field. The science classes were not what Roosevelt had hoped for, however. They required working in a laboratory and looking through a microscope. Roosevelt preferred to hike through the woods and gather his own specimens to study.

At Harvard Roosevelt joined the rifle club, the art club, and the glee club, which is a group of singers. He also played sports such as rowing, shown above. Roosevelt later wrote that his greatest moment at school was his invitation to join the Porcellian Club, a social group. He also worked on a college newspaper and became vice president of the Natural History Society. On June 30, 1880, Roosevelt graduated in the top 10 percent of his class.

1

Begin by drawing a long horizontal rectangle. The rectangle will be the guide for your drawing of a shell. A shell is the type of rowing boat that is used in races.

2

Next draw the three lines as shown. The lines meet at points at the sides of the rectangle. The bottom line curves down a little. The top line curves up a little. The middle line curves up a tiny bit.

3

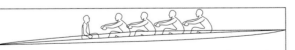

Draw the five small figures in the boat with a number of curving lines. Start with the figure on the left. This figure is the coxswain, or the person who guides the boat. The coxswain's arms are down. The other four figures are the rowers. They are leaning toward the coxswain. Their arms are extended.

4

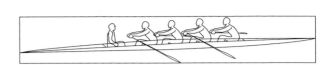

Next draw the oars in the hands of the figures rowing. The first and the third rowers' oars are visible in front of the boat. The second and the fourth rowers' oars are behind the boat. Then draw the small lines on the top of the boat, before the coxswain and after the fourth rower.

5

Erase the lines going through the figures' bodies. Fill in the details on the figures' heads. Draw lines for the coxswain's knee, collar, waist, and hand. Draw a half circle under each of the rowers' arms. Draw a line on each rower separating his legs.

6

Erase the guide rectangle. Then shade in the figures and the boat.

The Rancher

Theodore Roosevelt was a 19-year-old Harvard student when he met Alice Hathaway Lee, a 17-year-old woman from Boston. Alice was smart and she enjoyed poetry and art. They married after Roosevelt graduated in 1880. The two moved to New York City, where Roosevelt attended Columbia Law School. Roosevelt never graduated from Columbia. He entered politics, was elected as a New York state assemblyman, and began serving in 1882.

On February 14, 1884, Roosevelt lost the two women he loved most. In the morning his sickly mother died. Hours later Alice died, just two days after giving birth to a daughter, Alice. Filled with sorrow, Roosevelt left baby Alice with his sister Anna and headed west. He spent the next two years as a rancher. Roosevelt had purchased a cattle ranch named the Maltese Cross. The cabin is shown above. It was located in the Dakota Territory, an area that became several U.S. states. He tended his cattle and hunted with a few ranch hands. Roosevelt later bought a second ranch.

1

To begin drawing the Maltese Cross cabin on the facing page, draw a long rectangle.

2

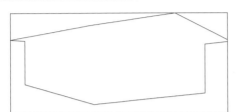

Inside the rectangle use vertical and slanted lines to draw the outline of the cabin.

3

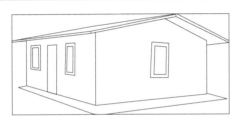

Use slanted lines to draw the cabin's base. Draw the edges of the roof with two thin slanted rectangles and a slanted line as shown. Add a vertical line to the cabin as shown. Beneath the right side of the roof add a slanted line and a small vertical line. Add rectangles for the windows and the door. Add a smaller rectangle inside each window.

4

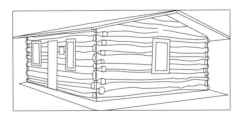

Draw a rectangle to the right of the door. Draw ovals and circles near the corners of the cabin for the ends of the logs. Draw uneven lines for the logs. Leave a blank space in the logs over the window on the right as shown.

5

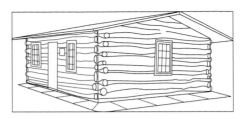

Draw the slanted lines on the cabin's base. Next draw vertical and horizontal lines to make panes on the windows. Last draw another rectangle between the two rectangles of the window frame on the right side of the house.

6

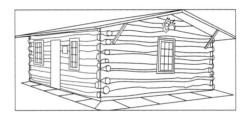

Draw two sloping supports that go from the roof to the side of the cabin. Then draw the shield shape and the deer antlers in the blank space above the window. Erase any lines that overlap the parts you just drew.

7

Erase all extra lines. Finish by shading the Maltese Cross cabin. This is how the ranch cabin looked after it was rebuilt in 1959.

Police Commissioner

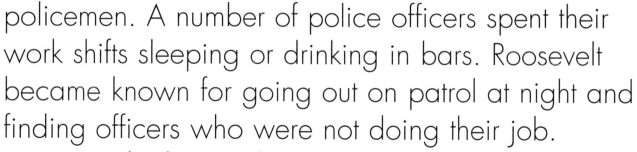

Theodore Roosevelt returned to New York City in 1886. In 1895, he was appointed as a police commissioner and the president of the board of the New York City Police Department, a position he held for two years. Roosevelt is shown in his office at top. There had been concern about the behavior of the city's policemen. A number of police officers spent their work shifts sleeping or drinking in bars. Roosevelt became known for going out on patrol at night and finding officers who were not doing their job.

Roosevelt also made sure that people obeyed the Sunday Excise Law, a law that made it illegal to sell liquor, or drinks such as beer or wine, on Sundays. This shut down pubs and beer gardens on Sundays. There was an outcry from many working-class citizens who used these places for social gatherings. At this time the two-day weekend for working people had not yet been created. Sunday was their only day off. However, Roosevelt still enforced the law.

1

Begin the drawing of the New York City police officer by drawing a vertical rectangle. Next draw a group of ovals that will be the guides for the head, neck, chest, and shoulders.

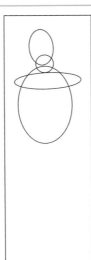

2

Use wavy lines to draw the police officer's hat and the shape of his face. Using the oval guides, draw the outline of his chest as shown. Add lines as shown for his arm. Draw his neck and collar. Draw his belt with wavy and slanted lines as shown.

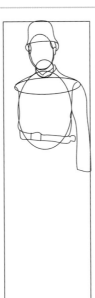

3

Use wavy lines to draw the police officer's other arm. Draw the shapes for his hands as shown. Add lines to show fingers. Draw the bottom of his coat. Use slanted and curved lines to draw the billy club, or stick, at his belt. Finally add the shapes for his legs and shoes.

4

Draw two curving lines on the police officer's hat. Draw his eyes, eyebrows, chin, mouth, mustache, and nose. Add a slanted line on each side of his nose. Draw seven curved lines on each sleeve. Draw a shield on his hat and another shield on his coat as shown. Add a slanted line below his belt and a curved line above his belt to show where the sides on his coat meet. Use wavy lines for his coat collar. Add buttons and folds to his clothes as shown. Finally add details to his shoes as shown.

5

Erase all the guidelines on the figure. Now you are ready to shade the figure you have drawn. Look closely at the image of the police officer on the opposite page and shade your drawing carefully.

Family Man

During one of his visits home from the Dakota Territory, Theodore Roosevelt spent time with Edith Carow, his childhood sweetheart. They became secretly engaged in the summer of 1885. Roosevelt's first wife had been dead for fewer than two years, so they felt they

should wait another year to marry. The couple married on December 2, 1886. They had four sons and one daughter together. Roosevelt enjoyed spending time with his family, shown above.

No matter what responsibilities required his attention, Roosevelt always made time to write letters to his children. In his letters Roosevelt praised his children for good behavior. He also let them know that he was unhappy when they misbehaved. In some of his letters, Roosevelt talked of his adventures fighting in Cuba in 1898 or hunting animals in Africa.

The Roosevelts spent their summers on Long Island. They lived at Sagamore Hill, which is shown above.

1

Begin your drawing of Sagamore Hill, Roosevelt's summer house, with a rectangle. The word "sagamore" means "chief."

2

Start drawing the outline of the house with an upside-down *V* a little to the right of the middle of the rectangle. Draw vertical lines under it. The left line bumps out at the bottom. Add the roof shape on the right side of the upside-down *V*. Draw the outline of the left side of the house. Now draw the right side of the house. Work carefully to draw all the lines shown. Draw two curved lines for the bottom of the house. Last draw the three chimneys.

3

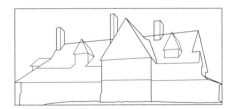

Add a small triangle on each side of the upside-down *V*. Draw vertical lines below the left triangle as shown. Draw a rectangle under the right triangle. Add roof shapes and sides to the right of both triangles. Draw vertical lines on the chimneys. Draw the shape and the vertical line on the left side of the house as shown. Draw horizontal lines and a slanted line across the house as shown.

4

Draw the details of the bottom of the house. Take your time and look at the picture and this example closely as you draw.

5

Draw two ovals on the left side of the house as shown. To the center section, add the slanted rectangle and the shape under it. Then draw the vertical and horizontal lines on the left and right sides of the house as shown.

6

Erase all extra lines. Draw small rectangles in the windows as shown. Add other lines in and around some of the windows. Add more vertical, horizontal, and slanted lines to the bottom part of the house as shown.

7

Erase any extra lines. Then shade in the drawing. The doors, the windows, the area under the porch, and the sides of the roofs and chimneys are the darkest parts.

Rough Riders and the Battle of San Juan Hill

On February 15, 1898, the *Maine*, an American battleship, was blown up in Havana, Cuba. The island of Cuba lies about 90 miles (145 km) south of Florida. At the time Spain ruled Cuba. Whenever Cubans protested the Spanish-run government, they were usually shot or sent to prison. President William McKinley believed that Spain was responsible for the bombing. The U.S. Congress declared war on Spain and the Spanish-American War began on April 25, 1898.

Theodore Roosevelt was then an assistant secretary of the U.S. Navy. He left his post to create a cavalry unit, called the First U.S. Volunteer Cavalry, to fight the Spanish. Americans called Roosevelt's unit the Rough Riders. On July 1, 1898, Roosevelt led his Rough Riders in a charge up San Juan Hill in Cuba, shown above. By the time they had fought their way to the top, the Spanish had fled. The Americans won the war soon after, which led to Cuba's independence.

1

Draw a rectangle. It will be the guide for your drawing of one of Roosevelt's Rough Riders. Newspapers also gave the group names like "Teddy's Terrors."

2

Inside the rectangle draw the outline of the horse. The back leg is missing its hoof.

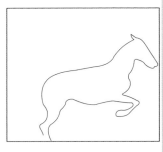

3

Next draw the legs on the other side of the horse. The back leg is missing its hoof in this step, too.

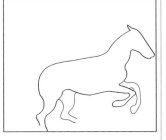

4

Draw the horse's tail and its mane. Then draw its eye and its other ear. Add small lines on the front legs to show the hooves. Finally draw the horse's saddle.

5

Start drawing the arm of the rider with the end of the gun in his hand. Continue the line down to the bottom of his boot. Finish drawing the leg and boot. Draw the body and finish the arms and gun. Add clothing as shown. Draw his head and hat. Last add details to the rider's face.

6

Erase the rectangle and any extra lines. Draw uneven lines for the grass. Draw details on the saddle and his clothing. Add the stirrup for the rider's foot. Add the reins on the horse's head. Add details to the horse's eye, nose, neck, and mouth.

7

Now shade in the horse and rider. The horse's mane and tail are dark.

Roosevelt Against the Monopolies

Theodore Roosevelt became governor of New York when he returned from Cuba in 1898. In 1900, he was elected as William McKinley's vice president. When McKinley was assassinated in 1901, Roosevelt became president. This was a

time when U.S. businesses were growing rapidly. However, some large corporations were harming small businesses, as illustrated in the cartoon above. These large corporations had created monopolies that controlled an entire industry. Since monopolies had more money, they could sell their products at lower prices and put smaller companies out of business.

When Roosevelt took office, J. P. Morgan was one of America's wealthiest bankers. His company, the Northern Securities Company, controlled the Northern Pacific Railroad. Northern Pacific owned most rail businesses in the northwestern United States. In 1902, Roosevelt had his attorney general file a lawsuit, which they won, to break up the Northern Securities.

1

The cartoon shows a small company, Tidewater Oil, trying to beat a large monopoly, Standard Oil. Start drawing the Tidewater Oil character by drawing a vertical rectangle.

2

Draw the shape for the body. It is barrel shaped. Add the oval for the head of the character.

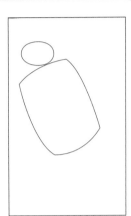

3

Draw a curved shape on the bottom of the body. Then draw an upside-down funnel shape on the head.

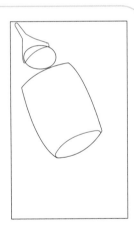

4

Add legs and arms to the character as shown. Both arms have cuffs. The arm on the left has folds. Add a hand to the arm above his head. To this same hand add a long, curved shape.

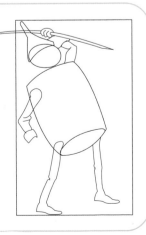

5

Add a hand to the arm on the left. Draw a book under the arm as shown. Draw curved stripes on the body of the character as shown. Add a collar on the top of the body. Add lines for feathers to the stick in his raised hand.

6

Draw the character's nose, chin, and jaw. Add lines for his ear, his hair, and the strap on his funnel hat. Add the shape for his eye. Write "TIDEWATER PIPE LINE" on the character's body.

7

Erase all extra lines. Now shade in your cartoon character. The Tidewater Oil Company was finally taken over by an oil monopoly.

The Great Conservationist

Theodore Roosevelt had a lifelong interest in nature. As he grew older, he became a conservationist. This is someone who protects the environment and natural  resources, such as land, forests, and waterways, so that future generations can enjoy them. President Roosevelt had the government protect more than 230 million acres (93 million ha) of land.

Between 1902 and 1906, Roosevelt created or enlarged five national parks. These parks include Yosemite Valley in the Sierra Nevada, shown above. Roosevelt also created 150 national forests, 51 federal bird reservations, 4 national game, or animal, preserves, and 18 national monuments. In 1908, he created the National Conservation Commission, which made the first inventory, or count, of America's forests, waters, and lands. In 1947, years after Roosevelt's death, the Theodore Roosevelt National Park, near Medora, North Dakota, was established in honor of the great conservationist president.

1

Start your picture of the Yosemite Valley by drawing a rectangle. Yosemite Valley became part of Yosemite National Park in 1906, while Theodore Roosevelt was president.

2

On the left side of the rectangle, draw the two shapes shown. Then add the two shapes on the right. These are mountains in the Yosemite Valley.

3

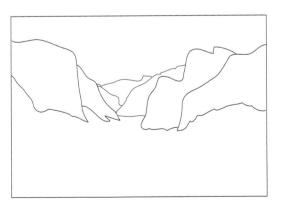

Use squiggly lines to draw the three shapes in the middle, as shown. These shapes are mountains a little bit farther away.

4

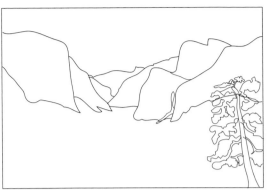

Draw two curved lines for the trunk of the tree in the lower right corner. Add shapes for the leaves and branches as shown. Add curving lines for the waterfall. Draw a line separating the rocks above the waterfall.

5

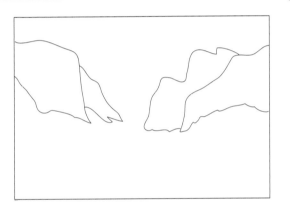

Erase any lines that run through the tree and waterfall. Now you are ready to shade in the drawing of the mountains. Notice all the different shades in the picture. Try to put as many different shades in your drawing as you can.

Building the Panama Canal

U.S. trade with nations in the Pacific Ocean and the Caribbean Sea increased after the Spanish-American War. To make it easier for large ships to sail from the Atlantic Ocean and the  Caribbean Sea to the Pacific Ocean, Theodore Roosevelt wanted to build a canal through a narrow strip of land in Central America. In 1903, the United States signed a treaty with Colombia, a country in South America, and paid $10 million for the strip of land that was called the Panama Canal Zone.

Roosevelt hoped a canal would allow ships to sail from the Atlantic to the Pacific in hours rather than the days it then took to make the 7,000-mile (11,265 km) voyage around South America. A military base in the canal would also give the U.S. Navy an advantage in sending ships to the Pacific. Construction began in 1904. The Panama Canal was completed by August 15, 1914. The SS *Ancon* and the tugboat shown above sailed on the canal that same day.

1

Start the drawing of the tugboat with a guide rectangle. A tugboat is a small boat that helps push or pull larger boats. It is useful in tight places like canals, where it is hard for larger boats to move on their own.

2

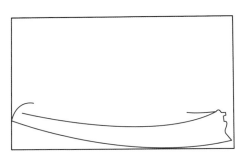

Draw the shape of the bottom of the boat, as shown above. Use an uneven line for the bow, or front, of the boat. The bow is on the right. All the other lines are curved.

3

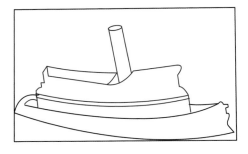

Draw the outline of the top of the boat. Add two curved lines to the boat. Use slanted lines and an oval to draw the smokestack. Add a curved line to the back of the boat. Add the shape to the left of the smokestack.

4

Add curved lines to the bottom of the boat, the smokestack, and the top part of the boat as shown. Add the shape to the back of the tugboat's top. It looks like half of a teardrop shape.

5

Erase the guide rectangle. Now add nine small rectangles for windows. Seven are on the middle part of the boat and two are on the top part. Then draw the shape for the smoke.

6

Now you are ready to shade in the drawing of the tugboat. The windows, the roofs, the edges of each deck, and the left side of the cylinder are all light.

Nobel Peace Prize Winner

In the early 1900s, Russia and Japan fought for control of Korea and Manchuria in Far East Asia. The Russo-Japanese War began in 1904, after Japanese ships attacked Russian ships anchored in Port Arthur, on the coast of Manchuria. Theodore Roosevelt feared that a victory by either country would allow the winner to take over China, one of the world's largest nations.

Roosevelt offered to arrange a peace conference between Russia and Japan. The talks for a peace agreement began in August 1905, in Portsmouth, New Hampshire. On September 5, the Portsmouth Treaty was signed by Russia and Japan. For his part in helping end the Russo-Japanese War, Theodore Roosevelt was granted the Nobel Peace Prize on December 10, 1906. This Swedish prize is given to a person who has made an outstanding effort to bring about world peace. The Japanese government also gave Roosevelt the sword that is shown above for his help in creating the treaty.

1

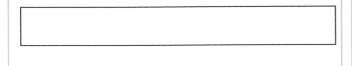

Draw a long horizontal rectangle. It will be the guide for your drawing of the sword. The sword was a present to Roosevelt from the emperor of Japan. Today it hangs in the North Room at Sagamore Hill.

2

Now draw the outline of the sword. Start with the curved shape to the left. This is the handle. Then draw the long curved blade of the sword. Notice the part that bumps out just after the handle. Work slowly to add the bumpy outline just to the right of the shape you just added. The rest of the blade is made using curved lines.

3

Draw the shape on the end of the handle. Then use lines and *X*'s to draw the details on the sword as shown. Use curved lines to draw the bands on the right side of the sword. The first band has three curved lines, the other three bands have two curved lines.

4

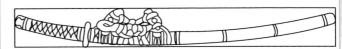

In this step you will add a lot of details on the shape to the right of the handle. Look closely at the picture and the sample drawing. Start from the top and work your way down.

5

Add small oval shapes to the right side of the sword as shown. The two at the right end of the sword are half ovals.

6

Erase the guide rectangle. Shade your sword. This sword was once used by a Japanese samurai. A samurai was an honored warrior in Japan. The special swords that the warrior carried signaled to others that he was a samurai.

Roosevelt's Death and Legacy

Theodore Roosevelt won a second term as president in 1904. He left office in 1909. In March 1909, Roosevelt led a hunting expedition to Africa with his son Kermit. They spent about a year hunting and collecting trophies of wild animals. In 1912, Roosevelt ran for president again but lost to Woodrow Wilson.

For the next seven years, Roosevelt wrote several books, including *Theodore Roosevelt: An Autobiography*. When World War I began, all four of Roosevelt's sons fought in Europe. His youngest son, Quentin, was killed in France on July 14, 1918. That year Roosevelt refused an offer to run for governor of New York. On January 6, 1919, Theodore Roosevelt died in his sleep at Sagamore Hill from a blood clot in his heart. Roosevelt had been a statesman, conservationist, and writer of about 35 books and thousands of magazine articles. He was also one of America's most popular presidents.

1

John Singer Sargent created the painting of President Theodore Roosevelt on page 28. Sargent was a famous painter. Start your drawing of Roosevelt by drawing a tall rectangle.

2

Inside the rectangle draw a large oval. At the top of the oval draw a circle as shown. On top of that, draw another oval. Draw the shapes for the arms as shown. Draw two straight lines in the bottom left corner. Last draw the outline of the bottom half of the figure.

3

Use the head outline to add the cheeks, the chin, and the ears. Add his hair using wavy lines. Use shapes and curved lines to add his nose, eyes, eyebrows, and mouth as shown. Use curved lines to draw the V of his open coat, his collar, and his tie.

4

Draw circles inside Roosevelt's eyes. Add circles around his eyes for glasses. Add lines to his nose, his cheeks, his chin, and his eyes as shown. Add the shapes for his mustache.

5

Draw Roosevelt's coat using the guides. Add his pants. Add curved lines for his shirt cuffs, the coat collar, a fold in his vest, and the edges of his vest and coat. Draw a line for his tie. Add buttons.

6

Use horizontal, vertical, and slanted lines to draw the details on the column. Then add the shapes on top of the column as shown. Last draw the fingers and bumps on Roosevelt's hand.

7

Erase all extra lines, including the rectangle guide. Now you are ready to shade the picture of Roosevelt. His hair, his tie, and the ball shape his hand is resting on are the darkest parts.

Timeline

1858   Roosevelt is born in New York City, on October 27.

1876–1880   Roosevelt attends and graduates from Harvard College.

1880   He marries Alice Hathaway Lee.

1882–1884   Roosevelt serves as a Republican New York assemblyman.

1884   Roosevelt's mother and wife die on February 14.

1884–1886   Roosevelt becomes a rancher in the Dakota Territory.

1886   Roosevelt marries his childhood sweetheart, Edith Carow.

1889–1895   Roosevelt is appointed civil service commissioner.

1895–1897   Roosevelt becomes a police commissioner and president of the board of the New York City Police Department.

1897   Roosevelt is appointed assistant secretary of the U.S. Navy.

1898   Roosevelt creates a cavalry unit, known as the Rough Riders, to fight in Cuba.

1898–1900   Roosevelt is elected governor of New York.

         Roosevelt runs for vice president on the Republican ticket with William McKinley. They win the election.

1901   Roosevelt becomes president after McKinley is assassinated.

1902   Roosevelt orders a lawsuit to break apart the Northern Securities Company and wins.

1904   Roosevelt oversees construction of the Panama Canal.

         Roosevelt is elected president of the United States.

1906   Roosevelt is granted the Nobel Prize for Peace.

1919   Roosevelt dies in his sleep at Sagamore Hill.

Glossary

anarchist (A-ner-kist) A person who stirs up trouble against the government.

assassinated (uh-SA-suh-nayt-ed) Killed.

attorney general (uh-TUR-nee JEN-rul) Chief lawyer for the government, who helps the president apply and enforce the laws.

autobiography (ah-toh-by-AH-gruh-fee) The story of a person's life written by that person.

campus (KAM-pus) The land and buildings that make up a school.

cavalry unit (KA-vul-ree YOO-nit) A military unit of soldiers trained to fight on horseback.

declared (dih-KLAYRD) Announced officially.

engaged (in-GAYJD) Promised to be married.

environment (en-VY-ern-ment) All the living things and conditions of a place.

expedition (ek-spuh-DIH-shun) A trip for a special purpose.

game preserves (GAYM prih-ZURVZ) Areas of land that are set aside for wild animals.

industry (IN-dus-tree) A business in which many people work and make money producing a product.

rancher (RAN-cher) Someone who raises cattle, horses, or sheep on a farm.

Spanish-American War (SPA-nish-uh-mer-ih-kin WOR) The war between the United States and Spain in 1898. As a result of this war, Spain gave Puerto Rico, the Philippine Islands, and Guam to the United States and let Cuba govern itself.

specimens (SPES-menz) Samples.

trophies (TROH-feez) Animals or fish that are often mounted for display after they have been killed.

volunteer (vah-lun-TEER) Having to do with soldiers who had jobs outside the military before the war.

World War I (WURLD WOR WUN) The war fought between the Allies and the Central Powers from 1914 to 1918.

Index

Web Sites

Due to the changing nature of Internet links, PowerKids Press has developed an online list of Web sites related to the subject of this book. This site is updated regularly. Please use this link to access the list: www.powerkidslinks.com/kgdpusa/troosevelt/